FRANCIS POULENC

DIALOGUES OF THE CARMELITES

Opera in 3 Acts and 12 Scenes

From the play by
GEORGES BERNANOS

Made into an opera with
the authorization of
EMMET LAVERY

This play was inspired
by a novel of
GERTRUDE von LE FORT

and a scenario by
PHILIPPE AGOSTINI
and Rev. Fr. BRUCKBERGER

English version by
JOSEPH MACHLIS

133006

RICORDI

LB 133006
ISBN 978-88-7592-553-6

CAST OF CHARACTERS

The Marquis de la Force - - - - - - -	*Baritone*
Blanche, his daughter - - - - - - -	*Soprano*
(Sister Blanche of the Agony of Christ)	
The Chevalier, his son - - - - - - -	*Tenor*
Madame de Croissy, Prioress of the Carmelite Convent - -	*Contralto*
(Mother Henriette of Jesus)	
Madame Lidoine, the new Prioress - - - - -	*Soprano*
(Mother Marie of St. Augustine)	
Mother Marie of the Incarnation - - - - - -	*Mezzo Soprano*
(Assistant Prioress)	
Sister Constance of Saint-Denis - - - - - -	*Light Soprano*
(A very young nun)	
Mother Jeanne of the Child Jesus - - - - -	*Contralto*
(Dean of the Community)	
Sister Mathilde - - - - - - - - -	*Mezzo Soprano*

Mother Gerald	Old	
Sister Claire		*Choristers*
Sister Antoine (Portress)	Nuns	

Sister Catherine - - - - - - - -	
Sister Felicity - - - - - - - - -	
Sister Gertrude - - - - - - - - -	
Sister Alice - - - - - - - - -	
Sister Valentine - - - - - - - -	*Choristers*
Sister Anne of the Cross - - - - - - -	
Sister Martha - - - - - - - - -	
Sister St. Charles - - - - - - - -	

The Chaplain of the Convent - - - - - -	*Tenor*
1st Commissioner - - - - - - - -	*Tenor*
2nd Commissioner - - - - - - - -	*Baritone*
Officer - - - - - - - - - -	*Baritone*
Jailer - - - - - - - - - -	*Baritone*
Thierry - - - - - - - - - -	*Baritone*
M. Javelinot, a doctor - - - - - - -	*Baritone*

Officials of the Municipality, Officers, Policemen, Prisoners,
Guards, Townsfolk.

DIALOGUES OF THE CARMELITES

ACT I

The action opens in April, 1789, as the first tremors of the French Revolution are beginning to shake the old regime.

SCENE I: THE LIBRARY OF THE MARQUIS DE LA FORCE
The Marquis and his son, the Chevalier, are discussing the Marquis' daughter Blanche — a sensitive, high-strung girl who cannot conquer her fear of life. Blanche enters, pale and overwrought. Her carriage had been stopped by a mob of angry peasants. Thoroughly shaken by the experience, she retires to her apartment to rest. The unexpected entrance of a servant suffices to throw her into a state of panic. The incident, trifling though it is, impels her to a step she has longed wished to take. She confesses to the Marquis her decision to become a nun. She no longer wishes to struggle with a world in which she feels herself to be a stranger.

SCENE II: THE PARLOR OF THE CARMELITE CONVENT
         AT COMPIEGNE
Blanche is interviewed by the Mother Superior, who explains to her that the Order is not a refuge from life and cannot give her the courage she lacks. What she seeks can be attained only through discipline and self-mastery.

SCENE III: THE WORKROOM OF THE CONVENT
Blanche and a very young nun, Sister Constance of Saint-Denis, go about their chores. Blanche chides Sister Constance for chattering unconcernedly even though the Mother Superior lies critically ill. Constance artlessly confides to Blanche a strange premonition she has had, that Blanche and she are going to die together, on the very same day.

SCENE IV: THE INFIRMARY
The Mother Superior is attended by the sub-Prioress, Mother Marie of the Incarnation. The Mother Superior is appalled at her own weakness. She has meditated on death every day of her life, yet now that she must face it she is afraid. In an affecting scene the dying

5

woman takes leave of Blanche and entrusts her to the care of Mother
Marie.

ACT II

SCENE I: THE CHAPEL

Blanche and Constance stand watch at the bier of the Mother Superior. Constance goes to look for their replacements. Blanche, left
alone with the body, is overcome by fear and retreats to the door,
where she is confronted by Mother Marie. The latter realizes that
Blanche has failed in her duty but, seeing how distraught the girl
is, accompanies her to her cell.

INTERLUDE

Blanche and Constance discuss the Mother Superior's death. Blanche
is baffled by the fact that the woman she had worshipped should
have found so mean an end. Constance advances an artless explana-
tion of her own. God gives each of us the death that fits him; but
sometimes, as in a cloakroom, there is a mistake. The Prioress had
received a death much too small for her. Which could only mean
that some little person somewhere, when his time came, would be
astonished at what a large death he was having, and how easily and
bravely he entered into it.

SCENE II: THE CHAPTER ROOM

The Community assembles for the ceremony of obedience to the new
Prioress, Mme. Lidoine, a plain-spoken woman of humble birth.

INTERLUDE

The Chevalier is forced to leave France. He comes to the Convent
in order to take leave of Blanche.

SCENE III: THE PARLOR

Both Blanche and her brother are constrained. He urges her to return to their father, who is now alone. Blanche, despite her love for
her brother, makes it clear that life in the Convent has wrought a
great change in her. Although aware of her duty to her father,
she now acknowledges a higher loyalty.

SCENE IV: THE SACRISTY

The Chaplain of the Convent informs the assembled nuns that he
has been relieved of his duties by the revolutionary regime and must
leave them. The Revolution reaches the Convent when a mob

6

gathers at the gate demanding admittance. An official reads the decree of the Legislative Assembly: all religious orders are to be dissolved. An older nun tries to comfort Blanche by entrusting to her the statue of the Little King. Blanche, overcome with fright at the sound of the *Ça ira*, lets fall the sacred image, which breaks against the flagstones.

ACT III

SCENE I: THE CHAPEL

The Convent has been pillaged by the mob. The nuns welcome the Chaplain, who has surreptitiously returned to them. In the absence of the Mother Superior, Mother Marie takes charge. She proposes that the nuns take the vow of martyrdom, but makes it clear that the decision can be binding only if it is unanimous. Each nun passes behind the altar and makes known her decision to the Chaplain. Blanche emerges with haggard face. The Chaplain informs Mother Marie that there was one vote against. The nuns have good reason to suspect whose that was. At this point, to their amazement, Sister Constance announces that it was she who cast the dissenting vote, but that she now wishes to reverse herself. The Chaplain grants her permission to do so. Thus Mother Marie's proposal is accepted. The nuns advance two by two — Blanche and Constance, as the youngest, come first — to take the vow of martyrdom administered by the Chaplain.

INTERLUDE I

The Carmelites, divested of their religious garb and led by the Mother Superior, leave the Convent.

SCENE II: THE LIBRARY OF THE MARQUIS DE LA FORCE

The room bears the marks of pillage and disorder. Blanche, dressed as a woman of the people, works as a servant in the mansion of her ancestors. Mother Marie, also in civilian costume, comes looking for her and tries to persuade her to return to the nuns. Blanche refuses, feeling that she is safer where she is. We learn that the Marquis has been guillotined a week earlier.

INTERLUDE II

A street near the Bastille. Blanche hears an old woman say that she has just come from Compiègne. She questions her and learns that the nuns have been arrested.

SCENE III: THE CONCIERGERIE

The nuns come to the end of their first night in prison. Sister Constance still believes that Blanche will return to join them. The jailer arrives and reads to them the decree sentencing them to death for crimes against the Republic. The Mother Superior gives them her blessing and places them "under obedience for the last time, once and for all . . ."

INTERLUDE

Mother Marie learns of the sentence from the Chaplain. She feels she ought to rejoin the Sisters in death. But the Chaplain reminds her that it is God who decides which of us shall live and which shall die.

SCENE IV: PLACE DE LA REVOLUTION

The Carmelites, led by the Mother Superior, go to the guillotine chanting the *Salve Regina*. As each ascends the scaffold, the voices are diminished by one. Presently only one voice is left, that of Sister Constance. At this point, from the other end of the square, Blanche makes her way through the crowd toward the scaffold. When Constance's voice is cut off, Blanche's takes up the hymn. She mounts the scaffold without a vestige of fear, achieving in death that victory toward which her whole life had aspired.

FRANCIS POULENC

Francis Poulenc (1899-1963) is one of the distinguished representatives of the present-day French School. He came into prominence, in the years after the first World War, as a member of the group of young French musicians known as "Les Six". Their spiritual godfather was the composer Erik Satie; their literary propagandist was Jean Cocteau. Only three of the six achieved international prominence — Darius Milhaud, Arthur Honegger and Poulenc. Under Satie's influence they endeavored to lead French music away from the grand gestures of nineteenth century romanticism. Satie preached simplicity, naturalness, freedom from every vestige of pretentiousness. This esthetic formed the basis for Poulenc's art.

From the first his music displayed an urbanity and elegance that were distinctively Parisian. It had about it the touch of the music halls, of the boulevards, of Massenet (has it not been said that there is a bit of Massenet in every Frenchman?) — above all, a humor and whimsy that imparted to it a special charm of its own. Behind his occasional clowning is a rich vein of lyricism that appears to best advantage in his moving choral works. Poulenc began by being fashionable with the chic audience that desires above all to be amused. But the underlying honesty of his music, its melodic distinction, its refinement and taste caused it to make its way with the big public.

Dialogues of the Carmelites is Poulenc's most weighty work. Written in the years 1953-55 , the opera reveals the composer at his most serious. The play by the Catholic poet Georges Bernanos afforded him a congenial vehicle for the deep religious sentiment which is a prime component of his make-up; also for that sympathetic handling of women's voices which distinguishes his vocal music. The disciple of Satie is evident in the sparseness of texture and the archaic-sounding harmonies moving in parallel motion; in the precision and quiet simplicity of the musical expression; in the avoidance of everything that smacks of rhetoric and bombast. The dramatic climaxes are projected through understatement. What fascinates the composer, clearly, is the drama of the inner life. Apparent everywhere is the lucid and elegant restraint which is part of Poulenc's heritage as a Frenchman; and the sensitive melodic line that underlines his position as one of the lyric voices of our time.

9

The work is dedicated to Debussy who, the composer stated, "gave me the taste for writing music;" and to Monteverdi, Verdi and Musorgsky, "who have served me here as models." The Russian master's influence on Poulenc's generation of musicians is apparent in occasional reminiscences of *Boris Godunov*. More subtle and harder to define is the influence of the Italians. Evident in the sustained and broadly soaring curves of the melody, this has been absorbed and transmuted by the composer's personality into something essentially Gallic.

The work received its première at La Scala, Milan, on January 26, 1957, and scored a tumultuous success. Almost immediately arrangements were made to present it in Paris, Cologne, Geneva, San Francisco and New York (over the NBC television network). Our age has not been overly productive of lyric dramas conceived on the grand scale. *Dialogues of the Carmelites* may well prove to be one of the significant operatic achievements of the mid-twentieth century.

J. M.

ACT I

SCENE I

The library of the Marquis de la Force, April 1789. A double door to the left; a little door to the right. A large fireplace. A window in the back. The furnishings are most sumptuous and elegant. As the curtains rises, the Marquis is napping in a large easy-chair. The Chevalier enters brusquely through the large door, which he leaves open behind him. He is visibly surprised by the presence of his father, but cannot hold back the question that bursts from his lips:

THE CHEVALIER

Where is Blanche?

THE MARQUIS

My word, you startled me! Why the devil don't you first ask the maids, instead of bursting in without a warning, like a Turk?

THE CHEVALIER

I am sorry, sir — will you pardon me?

THE MARQUIS

There is no harm at your age in being impulsive and brusque, as it is natural at mine to be calm and a little mellow. The unexpected visit of your uncle deprived me of my midday nap, so I was trying to rest a little while . . . or maybe dozing: But — why do you want your sister?

THE CHEVALIER

Roger de Damas, a while ago, started out from here but soon returned . . . or he would have found himself stopped by a mob of infuriated peasants. I have heard that they will burn the effigy of Réveillon in front of his palace.

THE MARQUIS

O well, let them burn it. When wine is plentiful and cheap, you may well expect that Spring will turn their heads and cause a bit of trouble. Never fear . . . It will pass!

THE CHEVALIER

If I dared to be flippant in your presence, or if I might make a feeble joke, I would respectfully suggest that on the subject of my sister's coach you may turn out to be a poor prophet. Damas himself saw the carriage surrounded at the crossroad near Burcy.

The Marquis de la Force, who had opened his snuffbox, shuts it brusquely without taking anything from it. As the Chevalier approaches, he holds him back gently with extended hand.

THE MARQUIS

The carriage . . . the peasants . . . If you must know, these are the visions that often haunt my dreams at night. You hear them talk about rebellion and even revolution! But if you have never watched a crowd in panic you have seen nothing, my son. All those faces with their features contorted . . . thousands and thousands of eyes . . . How well I recall the wedding of the Dauphin. Everyone was watching the fireworks. Suddenly some rockets caught fire and exploded. There you had the panic that can drive a crowd to frenzy. Your mother quickly locked the door of our carriage. The coachman lashed the horses; they bounded forward. Now the mob surrounds the carriage, soon the window is smashed by a stone . . .

The Marquis buries his face in his hands.

Just in time the soldiers arrived and came to our rescue. It was later that night, in the stillness of this house, your dear mother died — after giving birth to Blanche.

THE CHEVALIER

Monsieur, you must forgive me, for I should have known better . . . This is once again that I spoke like a fool!

The Marquis returns to his snuffbox. He taps the cover with the tips of his fingers, pensive.

THE MARQUIS

Bah! Look at me growing excited, exactly like you.

The Marquis remains thoughtful.

But my carriage is sturdy, my trusty horses are never afraid, Antoine has been with us for twenty years. I can assure you that your sister will come to no harm.

THE CHEVALIER

Oh, it is not her safety that worries me. But, as you know, Blanche is high-strung and inclined to be morbid.

THE MARQUIS

Blanche is only sensitive, and too intense. A happy marriage is all she needs. Oh come! You know . . . Any pretty girl has the right to be a little nervous. Be patient! You will yet have nephews as wild as ten thousand devils!

THE CHEVALIER

Mark my word: more than fear endangers my sister's health, perhaps even her life! It is not fear alone that causes her anguish. You must look beneath the surface . . .

THE MARQUIS

My! but you sound just like an old woman. Blanche often enough seems to be cheerful and natural. Sometimes she is even quite lively.

THE CHEVALIER

Oh, I am certain. There are times, I must admit, when she fools even me. I would believe the spell had been broken, if I did not see the sign of illness deep within her eyes.

THE MARQUIS

Soon enough, when Blanche and her companion will come to tell us they have returned, you will laugh at all your misgivings and she will forget her own.

THE CHEVALIER

You mean to tell me that Blanche once again had a little fright and nothing more? And nothing more! When it comes to my sister, the word "fright" fills me with foreboding. A girl so noble and proud — yet terror destroys her soul even as rot destroys the fruit!

THE MARQUIS

What utter nonsense!

Blanche appears through the open door, so suddenly that one is not certain whether or not she has heard the last words. The Chevalier cannot repress a gesture of surprise; but the old Marquis is in better control of his nerves and says in a most natural voice:

Blanche, your brother was most impatient for your return.

BLANCHE

My brother is much too kind to his little lamb.

THE CHEVALIER

You should not repeat at every turn a joke that makes sense only to us.

Blanche looks profoundly disturbed, but
she obviously has had time to take hold
of herself and forces herself to speak
playfully.

BLANCHE

I assure you that lambs are not accustomed to spend any time away from home. It is true that I should have felt at home in my carriage. But just a single window between my frightened self and all that howling mob — only one little glass, you may believe me, seemed to be a very poor protection. I must really have looked completely foolish.

THE CHEVALIER

Monsieur de Damas, who saw you at the crossroad near Bucy, told us you sat there behind your window looking perfectly calm and courageous.

BLANCHE

Oh! Monsieur de Damas without a doubt saw what he wished to see. So you think that I looked calm and courageous? Good Lord, it is with danger as with plunging into the ocean, which begins by taking your breath away, yet becomes most refreshing after you have gone in up to your neck.

She makes an effort to smile but, on
the verge of fainting, leans on the back
of a chair.

This morning at the Convent the service was extremely long. I am afraid it left me completely exhausted. I suppose this is why I am talking nonsense. If you will excuse me now, dear father, I will go to my room and rest a while before dinner. My! it grows dark quickly tonight.

THE MARQUIS

It looks as if there is a storm approaching.

Blanche goes towards the door.

THE CHEVALIER

As you are going up alone to your apartment, why don't you ask the servants for some candles. Nor should you stay there alone. I know the shadows of twilight make you sad and uneasy. When you were little, you used to tell me: "I die every night, only to be born again next morning!"

BLANCHE

There has been only one morning of Resurrection, dear brother, that of Easter. But every night of one's life is like the night of the Agony of Christ.

Blanche goes out without closing the door behind her, leaving the Marquis and the Chevalier baffled. The Marquis tries to reassure himself.

THE MARQUIS

Her fantasy is always in flight from one extreme to another. What did she mean by that remark?

THE CHEVALIER

I hardly think it matters. It is her look and her voice that pierce my heart.

Suddenly deciding to break the heavy mood:

I wonder if the horses have been fed. I will go and question old Antoine.

He leaves through the small door to the right. The Marquis resumes his nap.

BLANCHE

Off stage

Ah!

THE MARQUIS

Starting up

Is it you, Thierry?

Rushes to the door and calls:

What is going on, my boy?

A long silence, during which heavy footsteps are heard approaching,

THIERRY

Enters in the height of terror. He is a tall, simple-minded footman.

I just had lit the candles, when Mademoiselle Blanche suddenly came

15

into the room . . . I think she was frightened by my shadow on the wall. I had drawn all the curtains.

Blanche, livid, appears on the threshold. Her voice, her manner and her features display a kind of resolution and desperate resignation.

THE MARQUIS

Trying to be playful

My dear, I am glad to see it was nothing serious.

BLANCHE

With great intensity

Oh! Monsieur, you have been so very kind to me and such a loving father . . .

THE MARQUIS

This little incident can now be forgotten.

BLANCHE

Dear father, there is nothing so small or unimportant that does not bear the signature of God; just as all the immensity of Heaven lies in a drop of water. If you will grant me your permission, I have decided to become a nun!

THE MARQUIS

Become a nun!

BLANCHE

I think this decision must surprise you less than you would care to admit at this moment.

THE MARQUIS

Very gently

Alas! One should mistrust, when it comes to a young woman who is as virtuous as my daughter, all decisions taken in a moment of fervor. If you were not so proud, you would not be so perturbed by a cry.

Firmly

One should not renounce the world out of spite.

BLANCHE

Frightened

I neither hate the world nor despise it. For me the world is very strange, like an alien place in which I cannot live.

16

Breathlessly

Yes, dear father, I am quite unable to bear the strain . . . the fearful noise . . . the excitement. If my nerves were only spared the attempt, then you would see all I could accomplish.

THE MARQUIS

Deeply moved

My beloved child, if this is so, only your conscience can decide whether this attempt is more than your strength can endure.

Blanche throws herself at the feet of her father, who is still seated in the chair.

BLANCHE

Oh my father, let us end this game, I implore you! Pity my grief and let me hope that I shall find some cure for the dreadful torment that makes my life so unhappy. If I could not believe that our Lord is guiding my life and fate, I would die of shame here at your feet. It may well be that you are right when you say my attempt was not carried to the end. God will hardly hold it against me. I give my life to Him. I abandon all! I renounce it all! So that He may restore me to grace.

The Marquis, lost in thought, gently strokes his daughter's head, which rests on his knees.

SCENE II

Several weeks later. The parlor of the Carmelite Convent at Compiègne. The Mother Superior and Blanche are conversing, seated on either side of the double grille that blocks off the former's black veil. Madame de Croissy, the Mother Superior, is an old woman who is visibly ill. As the curtain rises she attempts clumsily to bring her armchair closer to the grille. She succeeds with difficulty and says, somewhat out of breath, with a smile:

MOTHER SUPERIOR

Do not believe this chair that I use is mine through rank and position, like the footstool of a Duchess. Alas! this is the wish of my loving daughters who take such good care of me, and insist that I revel in comfort. But it is not always easy to revive all those former habits that one has long ago discarded. And I can see that what should have been a remarkable pleasure, must remain for me only a dire necessity.

BLANCHE

How delightful it must be, Mother, to be so far along the road — the road of detachment — that one never is tempted to go back again.

MOTHER SUPERIOR

My poor child, through habit we are finally set free from all. But to what avail can it be for a nun to be freed of all, if she is not also set free from herself — that is to say, from her own detachment?

Sternly

I see that the severe rules of our Order do not seem to frighten you.

BLANCHE

They attract me!

MOTHER SUPERIOR

Very gently

Yes, yes . . . your heart is generous and noble.

Brusquely

What draws you to the Carmelites?

BLANCHE

Very humbly

Does Your Reverence command that I speak with utter frankness?

MOTHER SUPERIOR

Yes.

BLANCHE

Resolutely

Very well. The quest for a life that is heroic.

MOTHER SUPERIOR

Brutally

The quest for a life that is heroic? Or for a certain manner of living which you believe, quite wrongly, would make it easier to be heroic — would put it, so to speak, in the palm of your hand?

18

BLANCHE

My most Reverend Mother, I can assure you I have never harbored such desires.

MOTHER SUPERIOR

The most dangerous of our desires are those we call illusions.

BLANCHE

It may be I have illusions. In that case, certainly, I had better be deprived of them.

MOTHER SUPERIOR

Emphasizing the words

You shall be deprived of them! I must warn you of one thing more, my daughter. Everyone here is much too concerned with her own illusions. My daughter, all thoughtful people must ask themselves what it is we serve. And, after all, they are justified in asking us this question.

Violently

No, my daughter, it is not the purpose of our Order to mortify the soul, nor do we propose to safeguard human virtue. We are only a house of prayer! Prayer provides the only reason for our existence. Whoever doubts the force of prayer must regard us all as imposters and parasites. If faith in God is universal, should not the same be true of faith in prayer?

With great intensity

And so each and every prayer — even the prayer of a little shepherd who tends his flock — is really the prayer of all mankind. And what the little shepherd does from time to time, with innocent and trembling heart, all of us must do day and night.

Easily and calmly

Oh my child, our Order does not lean toward tenderness and pity But I am old and ailing, I am approaching my end — I can permit myself to pity you. Difficult trials await you, my daughter.

BLANCHE

Why fear them if God will grant me the strength?

MOTHER SUPERIOR

What God desires to test is not your strength but your weakness.

Very gently

You are crying?

19

BLANCHE

I weep far less for sorrow than for joy. Your words are harsh, but I feel that, even if they were harsher, they could never break the power that draws me to you. I have no other refuge but this.

MOTHER SUPERIOR

Our Order is not a refuge. The Order does not watch over us, my daughter. It is we who watch over the Order.

With an effort

Tell me, my child, have you by any chance already chosen your name as a Carmelite, in case we decide to admit you as a novice? I am sure you already have considered this.

BLANCHE

Very gently

Oh yes, Mother! . . . I should like the name Sister Blanche of the Agony of Christ!

The Mother Superior gives an imperceptible start. She seems to hesitate a moment, her lips moving; then her face suddenly expresses the firmness and calm of one who has come to a decision.

MOTHER SUPERIOR

Go in peace, my daughter.

Blanche genuflects and goes out.

SCENE III

The workroom of the Convent. Blanche and a very young nun, Constance de Saint-Denis, take the provisions and packages which the nun at the door hands them.

BLANCHE

Again those accursed lentils! They say the merchants in town are hoarding all the grain, and that Paris is without bread.

SISTER CONSTANCE

Oh! But here is the iron we thought was lost. We have been looking for it more than a week. Just see how the handle has been covered with flannel.

Gaily

Now there will be no reason for Sister Jeanne of the Holy Child to cry aloud while blowing on her fingers:

Imitating a shrill voice

"I reckon it is not possible to press with such an iron! I reckon!" I would always bite my tongue so as not to laugh, but I was so delighted. That amusing "I reckon" made me think of the country, and our village folk back in Bretagne.

Very gently

Oh! dear Sister Blanche, two months before the day I entered this life, we all enjoyed ourselves at my older brother's wedding. The peasants were assembled in front of the house . . . twenty young girls presented him with flowers while the violins were playing. Then we heard Mass and dined at the Chateau, and danced all through the night. I myself danced five country dances, with all my heart, I assure you. These simple folk loved me to distraction, because I was always gay — and I loved them with all my heart.

BLANCHE

Harshly

Are you not ashamed to chatter on like this, while our Reverend Mother . . .

SISTER CONSTANCE

Very gently

Oh my Sister, if I could save the life of our dear Mother I would gladly surrender my poor little life, such as it is. Yes, on my word, I would offer my life . . . But really, when one is fifty-nine, is it not high time for one to die?

BLANCHE

Severely

But have you never feared death?

SISTER CONSTANCE

I do not think so. Maybe yes . . . but very long ago, when I did not clearly know what it was.

BLANCHE

And afterward?

SISTER CONSTANCE

Good heavens, dear Sister! Life suddenly seemed to be so amusing, I decided that death must be the same.

21

BLANCHE

And now?

SISTER CONSTANCE

Oh, now? I no longer know what I think of death. But life stil
seems to me so very amusing. I try to do as well as I can whateve
I am told. But I always find it so delightful . . . After all, can I b
blamed if the service of our Lord gives me pleasure?

BLANCHE

In a harsh voice

Are you not afraid that God will weary of so much good humor?

Sister Constance looks at her dum-
founded, her childlike face contracted
in a sorrowful grimace. Then she says:

SISTER CONSTANCE

Pardon me, Sister Blanche. I cannot help thinking that you pur
posely came here to do me some harm.

BLANCHE

Harshly

Very well, you are not mistaken . . . In fact, I envied you . . .

SISTER CONSTANCE

You envied me? Imagine that! This is really the strangest thin;
I ever heard of! You envied me, when I fully deserved to be pun
ished for having spoken so thoughtlessly of the death of our Rev
erend Mother . . .

Very humbly

Oh Sister Blanche, since I spoke so very heedlessly just before, wil
you be so kind as to help me atone for being so foolish? Let u:
kneel and pray. We will offer both our poor little lives for the lif(
of our beloved Mother.

BLANCHE

Brusquely

How very childish!

SISTER CONSTANCE

Oh! not at all, Sister Blanche. Really, I think it is such a lovel;
inspiration.

BLANCHE

With an unpleasant laugh

You are making fun of me!

SISTER CONSTANCE

The thought came to me all at once . . . I do not think that it would do any harm. I have always wished I would die very young.

BLANCHE

Savagely

What have I to do with this comedy?

SISTER CONSTANCE

Very gently

How strange! The very first time I looked at your face, I knew that my wish had been granted.

BLANCHE

What wish was that?

SISTER CONSTANCE

That . . .

BLANCHE

Put down that silly iron and answer me, will you please!

Constance obediently places the iron on the table. Her pretty face is contracted with sorrow, but retains nonetheless a kind of childish serenity.

SISTER CONSTANCE

I will! I knew that God would do me the favor not to let me grow old and that we would die together, you and I . . . Where and how, I assure you, I never knew. And at this moment I still do not know . . .

BLANCHE

What a ridiculous notion! Are you not ashamed of believing that your life could ever redeem the life of someone else? Your soul is filled with all the devil's own pride. You — you — you must stop!

She stops short. The expression of astonishment on Constance's face gradually disappears, as though she were beginning to understand, without quite knowing what . . . She meets firmly the distracted look of Blanche, who finally turns her eyes away; and she says in a sad and gentle voice, with a kind of poignant dignity:

SISTER CONSTANCE

I did not think that my words would cause you pain.

SCENE IV

A cell in the infirmary. Marie of the Incarnation is at the bedside of the Mother
Superior, who is in bed. Throughout
this scene, the Mother Superior's manner and bearing will contrast with the
anguished and almost bewildered expression of her face.

MOTHER SUPERIOR

Short of breath

Would you be so kind as to raise this pillow? Do you suppose that
Monsieur Javelinot will allow me to be placed in the chair?

With great intensity

I find it very painful indeed to be seen by my children while I lie
so helpless, just like someone drowning who is pulled from the
water . . . And this at a time when my head is still clear.

With a certain irony

Oh, it is not that I wish to deceive my daughters! But when one
feels such a lack of courage, one should at least be able to main-
tain one's composure.

MOTHER MARIE

I had the impression, Mother, that your pains were entirely relieved
last night.

MOTHER SUPERIOR

It was only a lethargy of the soul. God be thanked nonetheless, I
no longer felt that I was dying. "To see yourself die" — that is
only a phrase that people use. Very well, Mother Marie, it is true
I am watching myself die! And there is nothing to distract me from
the sight! I am all alone . . . Alone and helpless, without the slightest consolation . . . Tell me please, frankly — how much time does
the doctor still think that I will live? Do not deceive me!

Mother Marie of the Incarnation kneels
at the head of the bed and gently places
her crucifix on the lips of the Mother
Superior.

MOTHER MARIE

He says your constitution is remarkably strong, and fears that you
will have a very long and bitter struggle. But God . . .

MOTHER SUPERIOR

Very harshly

God has become a shadow!

24

With great intensity

Alas! I have been a nun for thirty years, and Mother Superior for twelve. I have been thinking of death each day of my life, and now it does not help me at all . . . It seems to me that Blanche de la Force is late today.

With great agitation

After yerterday's meeting, does she still hold to the name that she has chosen?

MOTHER MARIE

Yes. If it please you, she would still like to be called Sister Blanche of the Agony of Christ. You seem to be deeply moved by this choice.

MOTHER SUPERIOR

It was mine too, long ago. Our Mother Superior at that time was Madame Arnoult — she was eighty years old. She told me: "You must look within your heart. Who enters Gethsemane never will leave it. Do you feel you have the courage to remain, until the end, a prisoner of the most Holy Agony?" It was I who brought into our House Sister Blanche of the Agony of Christ. Of all my daughters, there is none who gives me greater cause for worry. I have often thought of recommending her to your kindness. On second thought, and if God permits, that will be the last deed of my incumbency. Mother Marie . . .

MOTHER MARIE

My most Reverend Mother?

MOTHER SUPERIOR

In the name of obedience, I entrust you with Blanche de la Force. You will answer for her to me before God.

MOTHER MARIE

Yes, Mother.

MOTHER SUPERIOR

With great feeling and gentleness

You will need great firmness and clarity of judgment, and character as well; for these are precisely what she lacks, and what you possess in abundance.

MOTHER MARIE

It is very true. You see me clearly, as always.

A knock on the door

MOTHER SUPERIOR

She is here. Ask her to come in.

Mother Marie goes to the door, steps
aside in order to let Blanche enter, then
goes out. Blanche comes forward and
kneels beside the bed.

MOTHER SUPERIOR

With infinite gentleness

I pray you rise, my daughter. I intended to have quite a long talk
with you, but the conversation I just finished has left me weary. You
are the last who came to us, and for that reason the closest to my
heart. Yes, of all my daughters, by far the dearest — just like the
child of one's old age, and thus the one most exposed to danger,
the one most threatened. Ah, to avert that fearful danger I would
gladly give my humble life. Oh yes, willingly I would yield it.

Blanche falls to her knees once again
and sobs. The Mother Superior puts her
hand on Blanche's head.

Now, alas, all I can give is my death, a very humble death ... God
derives great glory through His Saints, through His heroes and
martyrs. He also reaps glory through the poor and the needy.

BLANCHE

I have no fear of being poor.

MOTHER SUPERIOR

Oh! there are many ways of being poor, down to the most miserable
... and that is the one to which you are doomed. Dearest child, no
matter what happens, you must not surrender your simplicity. Oh
my daughter, remain forever so sweet and pliant in the hands of
God. The Saints did not always resist temptation. They did not
rebel against their own nature. Rebellion is always the work of the
devil. And, above all, never despise yourself! God has taken your
honor into His keeping, and it is safer by far in His hands than in
your own.

With great tenderness

Now rise again, this time for good. Goodbye. I bless you. Goodbye,
my dearest child.

Blanche goes out. Mother Marie of the
Incarnation returns with the Doctor and
Sister Anne of the Cross.

Monsieur Javelinot, I beg you to give me another dose of this
medicine.

THE DOCTOR

Your Reverence cannot take any more.

The Doctor will remain to the end beside the bed, silent and watchful.

MOTHER SUPERIOR

Monsieur Javelinot, you know it is customary in our Houses that a Mother Superior says goodbye to her Community. Mother Marie, please try to convince Monsieur Javelinot. This drug or another — it does not matter. Oh! Mother, will you look — can I possibly show this face to my dear daughters?

MOTHER MARIE

Oh! my Mother, you should not think about us any more. Your only concern from now on should be with God.

MOTHER SUPERIOR

Who am I, wretched as I am at this moment, to concern myself with Him! Let Him first concern Himself with me!

The Mother Superior's head drops heavily on the pillow. Almost immediately we hear her gasping.

MOTHER MARIE

Almost harshly

Your Reverence is delirious!

To Sister Anne of the Cross:

You had better shut the window tight. Our Reverend Mother is no more responsible for what she is saying, but I think it is better not to scandalize your sisters.

Sister Anne looks faint.

MOTHER SUPERIOR

Ah . . .

MOTHER MARIE

O come! Sister Anne of the Cross, you are not going to faint like a silly little girl! Down on your knees and pray! It will do you more good than salts!

While Mother Marie speaks, the Mother Superior almost sits up in bed. She stares before her and as soon as she stops speaking her lower jaw drops.

MOTHER SUPERIOR

Mother Marie of the Incarnation! Mother Marie!

Marie of the Incarnation gives a start.

MOTHER MARIE

My Reverend Mother?

MOTHER SUPERIOR

In a low, hoarse voice

I just saw our Chapel empty and desecrated — the altar split in two.
There was straw and blood on the ground . . . Alas! God forsakes
us, God has abandoned us!

MOTHER MARIE

Your Reverence is beyond the stage where she can restrain her
tongue. I do implore her to say nothing that might . . .

MOTHER SUPERIOR

Say nothing! Say nothing! Does it matter what I say? I have no
more control of my tongue than of my face!

The Mother Superior tries to sit up in bed.

Despair clings to my skin like a mask that chokes me . . . Oh! if
I could only tear away this mask with my nails!

The Mother Superior again falls back
on the pillow. Mother Marie leans over
her, sees the closed eyes, hesitates a
moment and says firmly to Sister Anne
of the Cross:

MOTHER MARIE

Inform your sisters that they will not see the Reverend Mother today. At ten o'clock, recreation as usual.

Sister Anne of the Cross goes out. The
Mother Superior, who has heard everything, slowly raises her eyelids. Her
glance shifts restlessly, although her face
almost seems to be fixed in the rigidity
of death. Mother Marie turns about
brusquely. The dying woman and the
living confront one another. The Mother
Superior suddenly sits up and says in a
strong voice:

MOTHER SUPERIOR

Mother Marie of the Incarnation, in the name of Holy Obedience
I command you . . .

Exhausted by the effort, she falls back
again, gasping.

Ah, ah . . .

The door opens and Blanche enters as
though walking in her sleep. The
Mother Superior catches sight of her

28

and makes an effort to call her. Blanche
remains standing as if petrified.

MOTHER MARIE

Our Reverend Mother wants you to come beside her bed.

Blanche, haggard, kneels by the bed.
The Mother Superior puts her hand on
Blanche's forehead. In a whisper:

MOTHER SUPERIOR

Blanche . . .

She tries to say something and suddenly
chokes.

MOTHER MARIE

It is really an outrage . . . they should not be allowed to see her!

MOTHER SUPERIOR

Beg forgiveness . . . death . . . fear . . . fear of death! . . .

She falls dead.

BLANCHE

To Mother Marie:

Our Reverend Mother wants . . . Our Reverend Mother wanted . . .
would have wanted . . .

She falls on her knees, sobbing, and
buries her face in the sheets.

ACT II

ACT II

SCENE I

The chapel of the nuns. The Mother Superior lies in state in the center of the chapel. It is night. The chapel is lit only by six tall candles that surround the casket. Blanche and Constance de Saint Denis stand watch over the deceased.

SISTER CONSTANCE

Qui Lazarum resuscitasti a monumento foetidum.

BLANCHE

Tu eis, Domine, dona requiem et locum indulgentiae.

SISTER CONSTANCE

Qui venturus es judicare vivos et mortuos, et saeculum per ignem.

BLANCHE

Tu eis, Domine, dona requiem —

SISTER CONSTANCE
AND BLANCHE

Et locum indulgentiae.

SISTER CONSTANCE

Qui venturus es judicare vivos et mortuos, et saeculum per ignem.

BLANCHE

Tu eis, Domine, dona requiem —

SISTER CONSTANCE
AND BLANCHE

Et locum indulgentiae. Amen.

On hearing the clock strike, Constance gets up and goes to fetch those who are to take their place, leaving Blanche alone. Blanche tries to pray. She stares at the corpse. Overcome by fear, she

33

rises and goes to the door. The door opens, Mother Marie appears. Mother Marie notices that Blanche is deeply troubled.

MOTHER MARIE

What are you doing? It is your turn to be watching.

BLANCHE

I . . . The hour was over, Mother.

MOTHER MARIE

What do you mean? Are your replacements ready in the chapel?

BLANCHE

They did not arrive . . . so Sister Constance decided she would find them . . . and then . . .

MOTHER MARIE

Very harshly

And then you took fright . . . and . . .

Blanche makes a move to return to the casket.

BLANCHE

I did not think that it was wrong to go to the door.

MOTHER MARIE

Very gently

No, stay here, my child! Do not go back, I beg of you. A task left undone is better forgotten . . . think no more of it. Look! You are so upset! But the night is cool, and I think you are trembling less from fear than from cold. I think I will take you myself to your cell. And now, please, do not brood about this trifle. Go to bed, cross yourself and sleep. With my permission you are excused from all other prayers. Tomorrow your failure will fill you with sorrow rather than shame. It is then that you will be able to ask forgiveness of God, without the risk of offending Him further.

Mother Marie takes Blanche by the shoulder and leads her towards the door.

INTERLUDE I

A clock rings. Constance and Blanche enter; Constance carries a cross made of flowers, Blanche an armful of flowers.

SISTER CONSTANCE

With great calm

Dear Sister, I think that our cross is much too big. The grave of our poor Mother is so small!

BLANCHE

What are we going to do with the flowers that remain?

SISTER CONSTANCE

Very well, we will make a bouquet for whoever is chosen Mother Superior.

BLANCHE

Harshly

I really wonder if Mother Marie of the Incarnation loves flowers.

SISTER CONSTANCE

Very sweet and naive

Oh, how I wish —

BLANCHE

That she loves flowers?

SISTER CONSTANCE

No, Sister Blanche — but that she be appointed Prioress.

BLANCHE

Harshly

You always believe that God will act according to your wishes!

SISTER CONSTANCE

And why not? What goes by the name of chance is perhaps only the logic of God. Think of the death of our dear Mother, Sister Blanche! Who would have suspected that she would have such trouble in dying, that she would die so badly? One would say that in giving her this kind of death, our good Lord had made an error; as in a cloakroom they give you one coat for another. Yes, I think her death belonged to someone else, a death much too small for her, so very small that the sleeves barely reached down to her elbows.

BLANCHE

In a voice filled with anguish

The death of someone else? What can that possibly mean, Sister Constance.

35

SISTER CONSTANCE

It means that someone else, when it will be his turn to die, will be surprised that he finds it so easy, and that it feels so comfortable. We do not die for ourselves alone, but for each other. Or sometimes even instead of each other. Who knows?

Constance and Blanche go out.

SCENE II

The Chapter Room. Two doors: a large one to the left; a little one to the right, leading into the enclosure. The Community is assembled for the ceremony of obedience to the new Prioress — Mme. Lidoine, Mother Marie of St. Augustine. The room is vaulted. A very large and beautiful crucifix hangs on the center wall. Underneath it stands the Mother Superior's armchair. As the curtain rises, the ceremony of obedience is coming to an end. Each of the nuns kisses the hand of the new Mother Superior. A number of nuns are already seated on benches along the wall. Blanche and Constance are the last to enter.

THE NEW
MOTHER SUPERIOR

My dear daughters, I must tell you once again that we have suffered a great misfortune by losing our beloved Mother just when her advice and guidance would be essential for us. We have doubtless left behind us those calm and happy days when we forget too easily that we have no assurance against grief and pain, and that we are always in the hands of God. What the future holds in store, what fate awaits us, I do not know. I expect from Heaven, in its bounty, only those modest blessings that the rich and mighty of this world look down upon and hold in scorn: good will to all living things, endless patience and tender conciliation. Of all the virtues these are most fit for poor and humble women such as we are.
Oh, there are many different kinds of courage, and the courage of kings and princes is not at all that of little people. It would not enable them to survive. Many a servant will copy certain traits of his noble master, but they really suit him no more than precious spices suit a simple little rabbit. May I repeat that we are poor and

36

humble women who have come here to pray to God. Let us beware all the things that lure our roving hearts away from prayer. We must distrust even the joy of martyrs. Prayer is a duty—martyrdom a reward. When a mighty king in front of his assembled court motions to a servant that she may come and sit beside him upon his throne, as if she were a well beloved wife, is it not much wiser that she at first refuse to believe her eyes and ears, and go on working in house and garden? I humbly beg your pardon for speaking in this simple fashion, as I've been used to all my life. Mother Marie of the Incarnation, would you find a proper ending for this little talk.

Mother Marie hesitates. But she is not one of those who let themselves be asked twice for anything.

MOTHER MARIE

My Sisters, Her Reverence has explained to us clearly that our most important duty is to pray. Let us obey, not only with our tongues but with our hearts, the noble precepts of our Reverend Mother.

At a sign from Mother Marie all the Carmelites kneel.

Ave Maria. —

MOTHER MARIE
THE CARMELITES
THE NEW
MOTHER SUPERIOR

Gratia plena, Dominus tecum, benedicta tu in mulieribus et benedictus fructus ventris tui Jesus. Sancta Maria, Mater Dei, ora pro nobis peccatoribus nunc et in hora mortis nostrae. Amen.

The Carmelites rise and begin to go out slowly.

INTERLUDE II

The doorbell rings violently. The Mother Superior and Mother Marie enter rapidly from the right, Constance from the left.

MOTHER SUPERIOR

What is going on?

SISTER CONSTANCE

There is a man on horseback at the gate. He insists on seeing our Reverend Mother.

37

MOTHER SUPERIOR

At which gate?

SISTER CONSTANCE

The one in the alley.

MOTHER SUPERIOR

As he is so eager that no one observe him, he must be one of our friends. Mother, go and see him.

Mother Marie and Sister Constance go out to the left. The Mother Superior remains, her face impassive; only her lips move imperceptibly. Mother Marie returns in haste.

MOTHER MARIE

My Mother, the man is Monsieur de la Force, who asks to see his sister Blanche, as he must now go abroad.

MOTHER SUPERIOR

Send someone to call Blanche de la Force. The present circumstances justify our breaking the rules.

Calls back Mother Marie, who had begun to leave

I should like you to be present when they meet.

MOTHER MARIE

Hesitating

If your Reverence would kindly permit . . .

MOTHER SUPERIOR

You alone, and no one else!

The Mother Superior and Mother Marie go out hurriedly, each on her side of the stage.

SCENE III

The parlor. The curtain is half drawn. Blanche has her face uncovered. Behind the part of the curtain that is not drawn, Mother Marie of the Incarnation, invisible to the audience, witnesses the interview, her face covered by a heavy veil.

THE CHEVALIER

But why so cold and far away? Never looking up at me, and barely listening to what I say! Can this be the welcome you owe to your brother?

BLANCHE

God is my witness, I have no desire to cause you the slightest sorrow!

THE CHEVALIER

To come straight to the point: our father feels it is not safe for you to stay here any longer.

BLANCHE

Gently

It may be that we are in danger, but I feel safe — and that is all I need.

THE CHEVALIER

But you seem so greatly changed from the Blanche that I knew! There is something in your manner — you seem constrained and ill at ease.

BLANCHE

If I now appear uneasy, it is only that I am so very awkward. I have not yet become quite accustomed to live in happiness and freedom.

THE CHEVALIER

It may be you are happy, but I doubt you are free! It is not within your power to rise above the laws of nature.

BLANCHE

Oh come, you surely do not believe the life of a Carmelite conforms to nature?

THE CHEVALIER

In times such as these, there is more than one woman, formerly envied by all, who now — believe me — would change places with you gladly. If I speak rather harshly, Blanche, it is because I see before my eyes the image of our father all alone among his servants.

BLANCHE

With a gesture of despair

Do you really think that I am kept here by fear?

THE CHEVALIER

Or by your fear of fear. After all, this fear is hardly nobler than any other. You have to run the risk of fear, as you run the risk of death. True courage lies in taking just this risk.

39

BLANCHE

In a choked voice

From now on I am here only as the helpless and innocent victim of Almighty God.

With great simplicity

God will do with me according to His pleasure.

THE CHEVALIER

This conviction that you have does not excuse you at all from obeying the wishes of your father.

BLANCHE

When I took the veil, I was freed from dependence on him. I owe him only the love and due respect of my heart.

THE CHEVALIER

Blanche, when I first entered this room, you looked as if you would collapse from exhaustion. I thought I saw, in the glimmer of this feeble lamp, in a single moment, all of our childhood.

His face becomes gentle.

It is only because we were embarrassed that we came to blundering words that border on defiance. Could they have changed my little lamb?

BLANCHE

Very gently

Indeed they did . . . Oh! not at all in her affection for you! But it is true that the day of my taking the veil was a new birth into hope and courage.

THE CHEVALIER

Oh! Blanche, enough of all these futile explanations. Remember that our friends and all our family are now in flight. No one here would say anything against you if you were to leave and join our father. He really has no one but you.

BLANCHE

Does he not still have you?

THE CHEVALIER

It is my duty to serve in the army of our Prince.

BLANCHE

Very well, and it is mine to remain here. Why must you confuse me with doubt, as with a poison that destroys? Yet from this poison I almost died. It is true I have changed greatly.

40

THE CHEVALIER

You no longer are afraid?

BLANCHE

In a toneless voice

Where I am, nothing can harm me.

THE CHEVALIER

Very well, good-bye, my darling.

He goes towards the door.

BLANCHE

She turns back to him brusquely. At
these parting words she weakens and
clutches the grille with both hands. The
tone of her voice changes, as if she
were forcing herself to remain firm.

Oh, do not leave me so, in bitter anger and defiance. Alas! you are
so accustomed to pity and protect me that you find it difficult indeed
to grant me, instead, that respect and deep understanding which you
would grant to the least of your friends!

THE CHEVALIER

Blanche, now it is you who are angry. Are you really so resentful?

BLANCHE

I feel toward you only deep and tender affection. But I am no longer
that little lamb. I now am a daughter of Carmel, who will suffer
for your sake, and whom I now ask you to accept, once and for all,
as a companion in battle. For we are going into battle, each in his
own way; and mine has its risks and its dangers, the same as yours.

She has uttered these words with a
shade of childish emphasis and awk-
wardness that makes them all the more
touching. Marie of the Incarnation has
taken a step forward. The Chevalier
turns upon Blanche a long indefinable
look, and goes out. Blanche holds on
to the grille so as not to fall. Mother
Marie of the Incarnation comes forward
and says harshly:

MOTHER MARIE

Compose yourself, Sister Blanche.

BLANCHE

Oh my Mother, have I not lied? Do I not know what I am? Alas!
I could not bear their pity and contempt! May God forgive me! It
was weakness that sickened my soul. Ah, will I always remain a
child in their eyes?

MOTHER MARIE

Come along. It is time to go.

BLANCHE

I was proud, and now I shall be punished.

MOTHER MARIE

There is only one way to humble your pride, and that is to rise
above it. You must have courage.

She gently takes hold of Blanche around
the waist. They go out.

SCENE IV

The Sacristy of the Convent. Two doors:
the large one leads into the cloister, the
other into the enclosure. The Chaplain,
surrounded by all the nuns, finishes plac-
ing religious ornaments in a cupboard.

THE CHAPLAIN

My dear daughters, many among you already know what I am about
to say. I have been forbidden to perform my duties. This Mass
that I have just completed is the last. The House of God is empty.
I partake today of the grief of our early Christian fathers. Today
is a great day for Carmel. Good-bye . . . I bless you. We will now
sing together.

All the nuns fall to their knees.

Ave verum corpus natum ex Maria Virgine.

THE NUNS

Vere passum immolatum in cruce pro homine.

THE CHAPLAIN

Cujus latus perforatum unda fluxit et sanguine.

THE NUNS

Esto nobis praegustatum mortis in examine.

THE CHAPLAIN

O clemens!

THE NUNS

O pie!

THE CHAPLAIN

O Jesu fili Mariae. Amen.

The nuns rise. Blanche finds herself immediately beside the Chaplain.

BLANCHE

But what will become of you?

THE CHAPLAIN

Nothing different than I am at this very moment — an outcast!

BLANCHE

Overcome by fear

But if what I hear is true, you will be killed if they find you!

THE CHAPLAIN

They may not find me after all.

BLANCHE

With surprise

Will you go in disguise?

THE CHAPLAIN

Curtly

Yes. These are the orders we have just received.

Very gently

Dear Sister Blanche, your imagination is much too easily excited.

With great tenderness

Yes, my child, have no fear! I shall remain not far from this house. And I shall come here as often as I can.

On the threshold of the large door he makes a gesture of blessing her and goes out. Mother Marie with great calm draws the heavy bolts of the large door.

SISTER CONSTANCE

But can it be that priests are hounded like this — and in a Christian country? Have the French become such cowards?

SISTER MATHILDE

Harshly

They are afraid. Everyone is afraid. They infect one another with their panic, just as they might be infected with cholera or plague.

43

BLANCHE

As if in spite of herself, in an almost
toneless voice, of the kind one hears in
dreams

It may very well be that fear is really an illness.

SISTER CONSTANCE

Are there no men left in France to come to the defense of our priests?

MOTHER SUPERIOR

When there are not priests enough there are plenty of martyrs, and
the balance of grace is thereby soon restored.

MOTHER MARIE

In a low and hard voice filled with sup-
pressed passion

I feel certain the Holy Ghost has just spoken through the mouth of
Her Reverence. So that France may once again have priests, the
daughters of Carmel have only to give their lives.

MOTHER SUPERIOR

Very firmly

You did not hear me correctly, Mother, or at least you did not understand me.

Gentle and serene

It is not for us to decide if our humble names shall one day be
inscribed among the martyrs.

She goes out, followed by Mother
Jeanne. The nuns, dumfounded, look
at Mother Marie. The bell at the gate
is rung violently.

SISTER CONSTANCE

Someone has rung the bell!

SISTER MATHILDE

You must go at once and take a look at the little door in back.

The Chaplain comes up through the
little door. The muttering of the crowd
is heard off stage.

THE CHAPLAIN

I was almost caught between the crowd and the soldiers. I had no
choice but to seek shelter here.

SISTER CONSTANCE

You can stay with us, my Father.

THE CHAPLAIN

I would not wish to put you in danger. I have to leave you . . .
When the procession will enter the square in front of the City Hall,
the streets will be deserted.

The crowd draws closer.

SISTER CONSTANCE

Listen!

SISTER MATHILDE

Listen!

ALL THE NUNS

They are here!

THE CHAPLAIN

I think I have waited too long. What will happen to you, my daughters, if they should find me here?

A knocking on the door

THE CROWD

Why don't you open! Why don't you open!

The nuns huddle in a corner, with the
exception of Mother Marie. The Chaplain escapes through the little door.

THE NUNS

We will not! We will not!

The knocking continues.

THE CROWD

Why don't you open! Why don't you open!

A long silence. The murmur of the
crowd. A voice cries: "Open! Are you
going to open?" The blows rain upon
the door with ever greater insistence.
A plank of the door begins to give
way with a sinister crackling. Mother
Marie detaches from her bunch of keys
the one that opens the door, and hands
it to Sister Constance.

MOTHER MARIE

Go and open, my little daughter.

With a sure step Sister Constance goes
to unbolt the door. Four commissioners enter. Two remain by the door. The
crowd is held back by two guards armed
with long pikes.

45

1ST COMMISSIONER

And where are the nuns?

MOTHER MARIE

You will find them in there.

1ST COMMISSIONER

It is our duty to tell them the order has been issued that they be expelled.

2ND COMMISSIONER

He reads.

"Whereas it was decided by the Legislative Assembly, in session the seventeenth of August, seventeen ninety-two, on the coming first of October all the houses which at the present time are still occupied by members of religious orders will be at once evacuated by the same and will be put up for sale at the discretion of the proper authorities."

1ST COMMISSIONER

Do you wish to offer any objection?

MOTHER MARIE

How can we possibly object, when there is nothing left for us to decide?

Firmly

But it is really essential that we obtain some clothes, since you forbid us to wear these.

1ST COMMISSIONER

Good!

Forcing himself to adopt a bantering tone, for Mother Marie's great simplicity of manner awes him in spite of himself:

Are you then so very eager to throw off those silly old garments and to dress the same as everybody else?

MOTHER MARIE

I could easily answer you, it is not the uniform that makes the soldier fight. No matter what we wear, we shall always be humble and devoted servants.

1ST COMMISSIONER

The people have no need of servants.

46

MOTHER MARIE

But they have great need for martyrs, and that is a service we can assume as our own.

1ST COMMISSIONER

Mockingly

Bah! In a time of revolution, to die is nothing!

MOTHER MARIE

Scornfully

To live is nothing when life is thoroughly debased. Life has lost its meaning, and has no more value than your paper money.

1ST COMMISSIONER

Your words would cost you very dear if you had said them to anybody else but me.

To Mother Marie, aside:

Do you take me for one of those heartless ruffians? I was Sacristan in the parish of Chelles; our noble priest . . . I loved him like a brother.

Mother Marie's calm somewhat intimidates the commissioner.

Yet I have no choice but to howl with the wolves!

MOTHER MARIE

Please forgive me, but I must ask you to prove your loyalty and good will.

1ST COMMISSIONER

I will manage somehow to lead the patrol away. Only the workmen will remain here until tonight.

Aside, to Mother Marie

But beware of the blacksmith Blancart.

Whispering

He's an informer.

An extremely long silence during which the commissioners withdraw. The crowd leaves amid laughter and hubbub . . . Mother Marie goes to close the large door. The bolts drawn, she returns to the center of the stage. Tht nuns, dumbfounded, do not know what to do. Some are praying. Blanche, like a poor wounded bird, has dropped down on a little stool. Throughout the preceding

47

scene she had hidden behind the other
nuns. Mother Jeanne enters through
the little door of the enclosure.

MOTHER JEANNE

My sisters, our Reverend Mother is coming to say good-bye to us,
as she must go to Paris.

Mother Jeanne turns a pitying glance
upon Sister Blanche, then goes over to
a cupboard. She takes out the Little
King of Glory and hands it to Blanche
like a toy, saying gently:

My little Sister Blanche, every Christmas Eve, as you well know, we
carry our Little King into each cell. I trust He will bring you hope
and courage.

BLANCHE

Taking the Little King in her arms

Oh, He is so little . . . and so frail!

MOTHER MARIE

No! He may be little, and yet how strong!

There is an indistinct murmur off stage
as the crowd shouts:

THE CROWD

Ah! We'll win, we'll win, we'll win!

BLANCHE

She shudders, and allows the figure of
the Little King to slip from her arms.
It is broken to bits on the flagstones.

The Little King is dead!

Terrified, with the look of one who is
forever branded

And we have nothing left . . . but the Lamb of God.

The murmur of the crowd is heard off
stage.

ACT III

ACT III

SCENE I

The Community is assembled in the
chapel, which presents a scene of dev-
astation. Everything is covered with
straw and plaster; the grille of the
chancel is partly torn loose. A nun
watches near the door. Some candles.
The very modest civil garb of the
Chaplain is spotted with earth, his shoes
covered with mud; one sleeve is torn
the length of his arm. Mother Marie,
firm and calm, is surrounded by nuns.
Constance and Blanche are side by side,
Mother Jeanne and Sister Mathilde on
the other side of the stage.

MOTHER MARIE

Father, speak to them. I assure you they are fully prepared for the
pledge that must be taken.

THE CHAPLAIN

This is not one of my duties. So I think it would be fitting, in the
enforced absence of our Reverend Mother, that you yourself address
the Community.

MOTHER MARIE

With great decision

My daughters, I propose that we take the vow ... the vow of martyrdom, so that our beloved Order may be preserved and saved from
harm.

The Sisters look at each other without
enthusiasm.

I am happy to see you accept this proposal as unwillingly as our
Father in Heaven inspires me to make it. Yet, if we should really
offer our poor lives, we have no false illusions as to what they are
worth.

51

MOTHER JEANNE

> Brusquely

To what do we bind ourselves by this vow?

MOTHER MARIE

We surely do not intend to engage in any violent or indiscreet actions which would only be provocation and defiance. But there are legitimate methods for avoiding martyrdom, and we swear in advance that we never will use them.

MOTHER JEANNE

The trouble with all these special vows is that they threaten to divide our minds, and they may even go against conscience.

MOTHER MARIE

And that is why I have always believed that we should all recognize the great opportunity which such a vow must bring us. If there should be even one of you against this, it would suffice to stop me at once.

> For some time Sister Constance has been watching Blanche, first stealthily, then openly. Blanche seems very weary. One feels that from here on she will be the plaything of circumstances, and that in any case she will never dare to oppose her comrades publicly.

I would suggest that we decide this matter by a secret vote. Our Father Confessor will hear our answers in secret and under the seal of the Sacrament.

> Blanche's face visibly brightens. Sister Constance never stops watching her. Mother Marie turns to the old nuns.

Are you satisfied with this proposal, my Mothers?

MOTHER JEANNE

At least it sets our minds at rest.

THE CHAPLAIN

It would be best if you would pass one by one behind the altar.

SISTER MATHILDE

> To the nun beside her, indicating Blanche with a discreet movement of her chin

I wager there will be one vote against it.

> Sister Constance is quite close. We do not know whether she has heard. She

keeps her eyelids lowered. One by one the nuns pass behind the altar and reappear almost immediately. When Blanche reappears her face is haggard. Constance keeps watching her. The Chaplain approaches Mother Marie and says a few words to her in a low voice. Mother Marie, maintaining her calm, announces:

MOTHER MARIE

There was only one against. That is enough.

SISTER MATHILDE

To her neighbor

We know who it was.

SISTER CONSTANCE

Pale as death

It was I!

General stupefaction. Blanche begins to weep, burying her face in her hands.

The Father knows I speak the truth. But . . . but . . . now I am fully in agreement with all my sisters. And . . . and . . . I should like . . . I ask you to permit me to take this vow. I beg of you in the name of God.

THE CHAPLAIN

I so decide. Rejoin your companions. You will approach two by two.

The Chaplain puts on his vestments.

Sister Sacristine, open the Book of the Holy Gospel and place it here on the prayer stool.

The vestry nun places the Gospel on the prayer-stool.

First the youngest. Sister Blanche and Sister Constance, I beg you.

The contrast between the expression of Blanche and that of Constance remains striking. They kneel side by side and offer their lives to God. Blanche looks as though she is rallying her last ounce of strength. The other nuns mill about to take their places according to age. Taking advantage of the hubbub, Blanche flees.

53

INTERLUDE I

Three officers enter from the left. Almost immediately the Carmelites advance slowly from the right, led by the Mother Superior. They are in civil garb and carry meager bundles. The first officer addresses them.

1ST OFFICER

Citizens, we congratulate you all on your disciplined behavior and on your public spirit. But I must warn you, we shall keep our eyes upon you from now on. No more living in Communities, no more dealing with the enemies of the State — traitors doomed to fail — nor with priests who oppose the Republic — henchmen of the Pope and of tyrants! You will appear before the Court, one by one, and receive the card that will allow you once again to enjoy all the blessings of liberty beneath the watchful eye of the Law.

He goes out, followed by the other officers. The Mother Superior with a gesture holds back the Carmelites.

MOTHER SUPERIOR

Sister Gerald, we have to warn the priest as soon as possible. Last night when we met we agreed he would say Holy Mass this morning. But now it is very clear that this would be much too dangerous for him and also for us. Do you not think so, Mother Marie?

Sister Gerald goes out on the left.

MOTHER MARIE

I must rely upon Your Reverence from now on for all I should or should not think. But if I was wrong to act as I did, the fact remains that what is done is done.

She moves towards the left. On the point of going out:

Can we reconcile the spirit of our vow with all this caution?

She leaves.

MOTHER SUPERIOR

Turning towards the nuns

Each of you will answer to God for her vow and her conscience, but I will have to answer for all of you, and I am old enough to keep my accounts in order.

She goes out, followed by the Carmelites.

SCENE II

The library of the Marquis de la Force, pillaged and disordered, has become a kind of hybrid room. A low stove has been placed in the large fireplace. On top of it stands a common earthen pot. The once sumptuous furnishings have been partly destroyed. A folding bed stands in the middle of the room. Mother Marie, in civil garb, brusquely opens the large door.

BLANCHE

It's you!

Blanche looks at Mother Marie with a strange expression that contains both humble affection and mistrust.

MOTHER MARIE

Yes. I have come to bring you back. It is time.

BLANCHE

Haggard

Oh, but I am not free to go with you at present . . . But sometime later . . . perhaps.

MOTHER MARIE

No . . . not sometime later, but right away. Soon it will be much too late.

BLANCHE

Too late for what?

Mother Marie shudders. It is evident that she is disconcerted by this opening of the conversation.

MOTHER MARIE

For your safety.

BLANCHE

My safety?

Gentle and full of fear

Would you say I will be safer if I stay with you?

MOTHER MARIE

Firmly but gently

Down there with us you would run less risk than here.

55

BLANCHE

Anguished

I cannot believe you. In times like these, can there be any other safety than I have here? Where I am now, who would think of looking for me . . . when death only strikes in high places. But I feel so very tired, Mother Marie.

She trembles.

Look, my stew is burning! It was your fault! My God! My God! What will become of me?

Blanche, on her knees before the fire, lifts up the cover of the pot. Mother Marie also kneels and hastens to pour the stew into another pot. Blanche sobs.

MOTHER MARIE

Do not torment yourself, Blanche. See! No harm was done.

With infinite gentleness

Why are you crying?

BLANCHE

I cry because you are so kind. But I feel ashamed of my tears.

Gently imploring

I wish that they would leave me in peace . . . that no one would ever think of me again . . .

With sudden violence

Why do they reproach me? What harm have I ever done? I do not sin against God. Oh! fear is not a sin against God! I was born in fear, I have lived in fear, and I still do. All the world despises fear — so it is only right that I too should be despised. I have had this feeling since I was a child.

With deep and tender emotion

The only person who could have kept me from saying this was my father. He is dead.

In a choked voice

They guillotined him only a week ago.

She throws herself on the folding bed.

In this house that was his, I — so unworthy of him and of his name — what other role can I assume but that of a miserable servant? Yesterday, they slapped me . . .

With a kind of defiance

Yes, they struck me.

MOTHER MARIE

To be despised, my daughter, is not the real misfortune — but only to despise oneself. Sister Blanche of the Agony of Christ!

At this summons Blanche rises almost in spite of herself and stands upright, her eyes dry.

BLANCHE

My Mother?

MOTHER MARIE

I shall now give you an address. Remember it well. Mademoiselle Rose Ducor, 2 Rue Saint-Denis. You will be completely safe with her.

Emphasizing each word

Rose Ducor, 2 Rue Saint-Denis. I shall await you there, till to-morrow night.

BLANCHE

Mournfully

I will not go. I really cannot go there.

MOTHER MARIE

Nobly but with gentleness

You will go. I know that you will go, Sister Blanche.

A WOMAN
OFF STAGE

In a rasping voice and with exagger-ated emphasis

Blanche, have you done your errand?

Blanche escapes through the little door. Mother Marie, for an instant dum-founded, steals away through the large door.

INTERLUDE II

The scene shows a street in the neighborhood of the Bastille. Two old women and an old gentleman enter. There is a confused noise off stage, and the sound of a drum.

1ST OLD WOMAN

If you ask me, we've not yet seen the end of our troubles.

OLD GENTLEMAN

Yes . . . Life in Paris is becoming harder and harder.

Blanche enters. She carries a small basket filled to overflowing with heads of lettuce.

2ND OLD WOMAN

Oh, it's not any better elsewhere, Monsieur.

1ST OLD WOMAN

If not worse. Me, I come from Nanterre.

2ND OLD WOMAN

And I from Compiègne.

Blanche looks startled. She tries to overcome her fear and says in a profoundly disturbed voice:

BLANCHE

You come from Compiègne?

2ND OLD WOMAN

Yes, my pretty one. I left yesterday, with a wagon full of vegetables. They have a few bad fellows down there who are scared to death of each other and build up their courage by making enough noise for six hundred. Day before yesterday they arrested those ladies of Carmel.

Sees the agitation on Blanche's face and asks:

Would it be that you have relatives down there?

BLANCHE

Oh no, Madame. Besides, I have never been in Compiègne. It is only eight day ago that I arrived in Paris with my employers. We came from Roche-sur-Yon.

She forces herself to hide the nervous trembling that has taken hold of her. Her features show terror, and also something resembling a desperate resolution.

58

Suddenly gathering her courage, she slips away. The old gentleman is seated on a bench and rolls a pinch of snuff between his fingers. The two old women look at each other, shaking their heads.

1ST OLD WOMAN

You're a funny kind of servant, you sly one!

Everyone leaves.

SCENE III

The prison. The Carmelites are crowded together in the cell. Some old benches. A broken-down chair on which the Mother Superior is sitting. The barred window looks upon a dark courtyard. An unwieldy door. It is daybreak.

MOTHER SUPERIOR

Very calm and gentle

My daughters, we have almost come to the end of our first night in prison. Believe me, it was the hardest. And yet we have reached the end in spite of all. Tomorrow, I trust, will find us familiar with our new surroundings, and quite accustomed to the situation — which, besides, is not so new to us since, in fact, it is hardly more than a change of scene. No one could take away from us the freedom that we surrendered long ago of our free will. My daughters, it was in my absence that you decided to take the vow of the martyr. But whether it was wise or not, God will not allow that such a noble deed should now disturb your hearts and trouble your conscience. Well, I assume this vow. From now on I shall be bound by it too. I am and shall be, no matter what happens, the only judge of its fulfillment. Yes, I take the burden and I leave you all the glory, since I did not pronounce the vow myself.

With great gentleness

Therefore do not worry about it any more, my daughters. I have always answered for you in this world, and I have no desire at all to consider myself exempt from anything that may arise. So set your minds at rest.

59

MOTHER JEANNE

While Your Reverence is near us, we shall fear no man on earth.

MOTHER SUPERIOR

With ineffable sweetness

In the Garden of Olives, Christ no longer was master. He knew the fear of death.

SISTER CONSTANCE

And what became of Sister Blanche?

MOTHER SUPERIOR

I would not know about it any more than you, my little girl.

SISTER CONSTANCE

She will return.

SISTER MATHILDE

How does it happen that you are so certain, Sister Constance?

SISTER CONSTANCE

Because . . .

She stops, disconcerted.

Because . . .

Then in great confusion but unable to retract what she has said

Because of a dream that I had!

All the Carmelites, with the exception of the Mother Superior, burst into laughter. The door is suddenly opened and the jailer enters, displaying a document.

THE JAILER

He reads.

"The Revolutionary Tribunal declares that the former Carmelite nuns, who reside in Compiègne, Department of l'Oise, Madeleine Lidoine, Anne Pellerat, Madeleine Touret, Marie-Anne Hanniset, Marie-Anne Piedcourt, Marie-Anne Brideau, Marie Cyprienne Brare, Rose Chrétien, Marie Dufour, Angélique Roussel, Marie-Gabrielle Trézelle, Marie-Geneviève Meunier, Catherine Soiron, Thérèse Soiron, Elizabeth Vezolot, gathered together unlawfully in secret meetings against the Revolution, and engaged in correspondence that was fanatical, spreading writings opposed to freedom. Whereas they constitute a body of rebels, openly seditious, who nourish in their hearts the desire and the criminal hope to see the people of France once more in the chains of tyrants, to see liberty drowned in the torrents of blood which their treacherous plots and shameful designs have brought about in the name of God . . . the Revolutionary Tribunal in consequence has decided that all the afore-mentioned are condemned to death."

The jailer rolls up the document. The
nuns lower their heads. The jailer leaves.

MOTHER SUPERIOR

My daughters, I wanted to save you with all my heart. Yes, I would have wished you had been spared this sacrifice. For, ever since the day that I met you, I have loved you like a mother; and would a mother willingly see the sacrifice of her children, were it even for the King himself? If I have done badly, God will attend to it. Such as I am, you are all I possess; I am hardly one of those who empties her wealth out of the window. It does not matter, my daughters . . . there is nothing left but to die!

With infinite gentleness

God be blessed, who decreed the punishment we will suffer together, like the last celebration of our beloved Community. My daughters, I must now solemnly place you under obedience for the last time . . . once and for all, with my maternal blessing on you forever.

INTERLUDE III

The Chaplain enters brusquely. Mother
Marie, who had been waiting for him,
comes out of the shadows.

THE CHAPLAIN
They have been condemned to death.

MOTHER MARIE
All of them?

THE CHAPLAIN
All of them!

MOTHER MARIE
God! And —

61

THE CHAPLAIN

It will surely be today or tomorrow . . .

Mother Marie turns aside.

What are you doing, Mother?

MOTHER MARIE

I cannot let them die without me!

THE CHAPLAIN

Of what importance is your wish in this matter? God rejects or chooses whom he pleases.

MOTHER MARIE

I took the martyr's vow . . .

THE CHAPLAIN

It was God to whom you swore it — it is to Him you will answer for your pledge, and not to your companions.

Very gently

If it pleases Him to release you, He is only taking back that which is His.

MOTHER MARIE

I am dishonored! At the last their gaze will seek me in vain.

THE CHAPLAIN

With great gentleness

Think only of His gaze, on which you should fasten your own.

They go out.

SCENE IV

Place de la Révolution. On the right, the Carmelites finish descending from tumbrels. As the curtain rises, old Mother Jeanne is being helped down. Constance is the last one; she leaps down almost joyfully. Then the Carmelites, with the Mother Superior at their head, make their way to the scaffold. In the first row of the dense and restless crowd may be seen the Chaplain, wearing a cap of Liberty. He mur-

murs the absolution, makes a furtive
sign of the cross as the first Carmelites
ascend the scaffold, then quickly disappears. The chanting of the Carmelites is heard above the din of the crowd:

MOTHER SUPERIOR
AND
THE CARMALITES

> Salve Regina, mater misericordiae, vita, dulcedo et spes nostra salve.
> Ad te clamamus exsules filii Hevae, ad te suspiramus, gementes et
> flentes in hac lacrimarum valle. Eia ergo, advocata nostra, illos tuos
> misericordes oculos ad nos converte.

The Salve Regina is repeated, punctu-
ated by the dull rumble of the guillotine. We see only the base of the scaffold, which the Sisters mount one by
one. Their voices are clear and very
firm. But as each disappears, the chorus
is reduced. After the Mother Superior
is taken, the chanting is carried on by
seven voices, six, five, four.

SISTER CONSTANCE
SISTER MATHILDE
A CARMELITE
MOTHER JEANNE

> Et Jesum benedictum fructum ventris tui, nobis post hoc exsilium
> ostende.

Finally only two voices are left:

SISTER CONSTANCE
AND
MOTHER JEANNE

> O clemens, o pia, o dulcis Virgo Maria.

Then — only one, that of Sister Constance:

SISTER CONSTANCE

> O clemens, o pia,

But at this moment, issuing from another corner of the square, Blanche
makes her way through the crowd in
which she has been lost. Her face is
free from every vestige of fear. Constance catches sight of her friend, and
her face becomes radiant with happiness. She stops short for a brief moment, then resumes her journey to the
scaffold, with a gentle smile to Blanche.

63

O dulcis Virgo Ma—

Incredibly calm, Blanche steps forward,
amid the stupefaction of the crowd,
and mounts the scaffold. She takes up
the hymn at the point where Constance
had been cut off. Her voice sounds even
purer and more resolute than the others,
yet with something childlike in it.

BLANCHE

Deo Patri sit gloria et Filio qui a mortuis surrexit ac Paraclito. In
saeculorum saecula. In saeculorum—

The crowd begins to disperse.

CURTAIN